RECONSTRUCTION

History SparkNotes

SPARKNOTES is a registered trademark of SparkNotes LLC

Spark Educational Publishing
A Division of Barnes & Noble Publishing
120 Fifth Avenue
New York, NY 10011
www.sparknotes.com

ISBN 1-4114-0423-8

Please submit all comments and questions or report errors to *www.sparknotes.com/errors*.

Printed and bound in the United States

CONTENTS

Overview

OVERVIEW

B
y the end of the Civil War, the South was in a state of political upheaval, social disorder, and economic decay. The Union's tactics of total war destroyed southern crops, plantations, and entire cities, and hundreds of thousands of emancipated slaves rushed to Union lines as their masters fled the oncoming Union army. Inflation became so severe that by the end of the war a loaf of bread cost several hundred Confederate dollars. Thousands of southerners starved to death, and many who did not starve lost everything they owned: clothing, homes, land, and slaves. As a result, by 1865, policymakers in Washington had the nearly impossible task of southern Reconstruction.

Reconstruction encompassed three major initiatives: restoration of the Union, transformation of southern society, and enactment of progressive legislation favoring the rights of freed slaves. President Abraham Lincoln's Proclamation of Amnesty and Reconstruction—issued in 1863, two years before the war even ended—mapped out the first of these initiatives, his Ten-Percent Plan. Under the plan, each southern state would be readmitted to the Union after 10 percent of its voting population had pledged future loyalty to the United States, and all Confederates except high-ranking government and military officials would be pardoned. After Lincoln was assassinated in 1865, President Andrew Johnson adopted the Ten-Percent Plan and pardoned thousands of Confederate officials. Radical Republicans in Congress, however, called for harsher measures, demanding a loyalty oath from 50 percent of each state's voting population rather than just 10 percent. Although such points of contention existed, both presidents and Congress agreed on one major point—that the southern states needed to abolish slavery in their new state constitutions before being readmitted to the Union.

The Radical Republicans also believed that southern society would have to be completely transformed to ensure that the South would not try to secede again. The Radicals therefore attempted to reshape the South by enfranchising blacks, putting Unionist and pro-Republican governments in southern legislatures, and punishing southern planter elites, whom many politicians held responsible for the Civil War. As "carpetbaggers" (northerners who moved to the South after the war) and "scalawags" (white Unionists and

I

Republicans in the South) streamed into the South, southerners denounced them as traitors and falsely accused many of corruption. However, through organizations like the congressionally approved Freedmen's Bureau, the U.S. government did manage to distribute confiscated lands to former slaves and poor whites as well as help improve education and sanitation and foster industrial growth in rebuilt southern cities.

Ultimately, the most important part of Reconstruction was the push to secure rights for former slaves. Radical Republicans, aware that newly freed slaves would face insidious racism, passed a series of progressive laws and amendments in Congress that protected blacks' rights under federal and constitutional law. The Thirteenth Amendment abolished slavery, the Civil Rights Act of 1866 and the Fourteenth Amendment granted blacks citizenship, the Fifteenth Amendment gave black men the right to vote, and the Civil Rights Act of 1875 attempted to ban racial discrimination in public places.

Reconstruction was a mixed success. By the end of the era, the North and South were once again reunited, and all southern state legislatures had abolished slavery in their constitutions. Reconstruction also laid to a rest the debate of states' rights vs. federalism, which had been a pressing issue since the late 1790s. But Reconstruction failed in most other ways. When President Rutherford B. Hayes ordered federal troops to leave the South in 1877, former Confederate officials and slave owners gradually returned to power. Southern state legislatures quickly passed "black codes," imposed voter qualifications, and allowed the sharecropping system to thrive, ensuring that the standard of living did not improve for freed slaves. A conservative Supreme Court aided southern Democrats by effectively repealing the Fourteenth and Fifteenth Amendments as well as the Civil Rights Act of 1875. By 1877, northerners were tired of Reconstruction, and violations of blacks' civil rights were essentially going ignored. Ultimately, the rights promised to blacks during Reconstruction would not be granted fully for almost another century.

Summary of Events

The Ten-Percent Plan

The process of reconstructing the Union began in 1863, two years before the Confederacy formally surrendered. After major Union victories at Gettysburg and Vicksburg, **Abraham Lincoln** issued the **Proclamation of Amnesty and Reconstruction** in which he outlined his **Ten-Percent Plan**. The plan stipulated that each secessionist state had to redraft its constitution and could reenter the Union only after 10 percent of its eligible voters pledged an oath of allegiance to the United States.

The Wade-Davis Bill and the Freedmen's Bureau

Many **Radical Republicans** believed that Lincoln's plan was too lenient: they wanted to punish the South for secession from the Union, transform southern society, and safeguard the rights of former slaves. As an alternative to the Ten-Percent Plan, Radical Republicans and their moderate Republican allies passed the **Wade-Davis Bill** in 1864. Under the bill, states could be readmitted to the Union only after 50 percent of voters took an oath of allegiance to the Union. Lincoln pocket-vetoed the bill, however, effectively killing it by refusing to sign it before Congress went into recess. Congress did successfully create the **Freedmen's Bureau**, which helped distribute food, supplies, and land to the new population of freed slaves.

Presidential Reconstruction

On April 14, 1865, **John Wilkes Booth** assassinated President Lincoln in Ford's Theatre in Washington, D.C., and Vice President **Andrew Johnson** became president. **Presidential Reconstruction** under Johnson readmitted the southern states using Lincoln's Ten-Percent Plan and granted all southerners full pardons, including thousands of wealthy planters and former Confederate officials. Johnson also ordered the Freedmen's Bureau to return all confiscated lands to their original owners. While Congress was in recess, Johnson approved new state constitutions for secessionist states—many written by ex-Confederate officials—and declared Reconstruction complete in December 1865.

PROGRESSIVE LEGISLATION FOR BLACKS

Although Johnson vetoed Congress's attempt to renew the charter of the Freedmen's Bureau in 1866, Congress was successful in overriding Johnson's veto on its second try, and the bureau's charter was renewed. They also passed the **Civil Rights Act of 1866**, which granted newly emancipated blacks the right to sue, the right to serve on juries, and several other legal rights. Although Johnson vetoed this bill as well, Congress was able to muster enough votes to override it. The Radical Republicans also passed the **Thirteenth Amendment**, which abolished slavery, and the **Fourteenth Amendment**, which made freed slaves U.S. citizens.

JOHNSON'S "SWING AROUND THE CIRCLE"

Many southerners reacted violently to the passage by Congress of the Civil Rights Act of 1866 and the two amendments. White supremacists in Tennessee formed the **Ku Klux Klan**, a secret organization meant to terrorize southern blacks and "keep them in their place." **Race riots** and **mass murders** of former slaves occurred in Memphis and New Orleans that same year.

Johnson blamed Congress for the violence and went on what he called a **"Swing Around the Circle,"** touring the country to speak out against Republicans and encourage voters to elect Democrats to Congress. However, many of Johnson's speeches were so abrasive—and even racist—that he ended up convincing more people to vote *against* his party in the midterm elections of 1866.

RADICAL RECONSTRUCTION

The Congress that convened in 1867, which was far more radical than the previous one, wasted no time executing its own plan for the **Radical Reconstruction** of the South. The **First Reconstruction Act** in 1867 divided the South into five conquered districts, each of which would be governed by the U.S. military until a new government was established. Republicans also specified that states would have to enfranchise former slaves before readmission to the Union. To enforce this order, Congress passed the **Second Reconstruction Act**, putting the military in charge of southern voter registration. They also passed the **Fifteenth Amendment**, giving all American men—including former slaves—the right to vote.

JOHNSON'S IMPEACHMENT

In an effort to limit Johnson's executive powers, Congress passed the **Tenure of Office Act** in 1867, which required the president to consult with the House and Senate before removing any congressionally appointed cabinet members. Radicals took this measure in an attempt to protect Secretary of War **Edwin M. Stanton**, a carryover from Lincoln's cabinet and a crucial figure in military Reconstruction. When Johnson ignored the Tenure of Office Act and fired Stanton, Republicans in the House impeached him by a vote of 126–47. After a tense trial, the Senate voted to acquit the president by a margin of only one vote.

The Black Codes and Ku Klux Klan

Despite sweeping rights legislation by Radical Republicans in Congress, southern whites did everything in their power to limit the rights of their former slaves. During Presidential Reconstruction, white supremacist Congressmen passed a series of laws called the **black codes**, which denied blacks the right to make contracts, testify against whites, marry white women, be unemployed, and even loiter in public places. Violence by the Ku Klux Klan became so common that Congress had to pass the **Ku Klux Klan Act** in 1871 to authorize military protection for blacks.

Carpetbaggers, Scalawags, and Sharecroppers

Countless **carpetbaggers** (northerners who moved to the South after the war) and **scalawags** (white Unionists and Republicans in the South) flocked to the South during Reconstruction and exerted significant influence there. Although in many respects they achieved their goals of modernizing and Republicanizing the South, they eventually were driven out by Democratic state politicians in the mid-1870s.

Most former slaves in the South, meanwhile, became **sharecroppers** during the Reconstruction period, leasing plots of land from their former masters in exchange for a percentage of the crop yield. By 1880, more than 80 percent of southern blacks had become sharecroppers.

Grant's Presidency

To the Radicals' delight, Johnson finally left the White House in 1868, when Republican **Ulysses S. Grant** was elected president. Grant's inexperience, however, proved to be a liability that ultimately ended Radical Reconstruction. Because Grant had difficulty saying no, many of his cabinet posts and appointments ended up being filled by corrupt, incompetent men who were no more than spoils-seekers.

SUMMARY OF EVENTS

As a result, scandal after scandal rocked Grant's administration and damaged his reputation. In 1869, reporters uncovered a scheme by millionaires Jim Fisk and Jay Gould to corner the gold market by artificially inflating **gold prices**. Schuyler Colfax, vice president at the time, was forced to resign for his complicity in the **Crédit Mobilier scandal** in 1872. The president lost even more credibility during his second term, when his personal secretary helped embezzle millions of dollars from the U.S. Treasury as a member of the **Whiskey Ring**.

LIBERAL REPUBLICANS AND THE ELECTION OF 1872

The discovery of new scandals split the Republican Party in 1872, as reform-minded **Liberal Republicans** broke from the ranks of moderates and radicals. The Liberal Republicans wanted to institute reform, downsize the federal government, and bring a swift end to Reconstruction. They nominated *New York Tribune* editor **Horace Greeley** as their party's presidential candidate (he agreed to run on the Democratic Party's ticket as well). Though already marred by scandal, Grant easily defeated Greeley by more than 200 electoral votes and 700,000 popular votes.

THE DEPRESSION OF 1873

In 1873, the postwar economic bubble in the United States finally burst. Overspeculation in the railroad industry, manufacturing, and a flood of Americans taking out bad bank loans slid the economy into the worst **depression** in American history. Millions lost their jobs, and unemployment climbed as high as 15 percent. Many blacks, landless whites, and immigrants from both North and South suffered greatly, demanding relief from the federal government. Republicans, refusing to give in to demands to print more paper money, instead withdrew money from the economy by passing the **Resumption Act of 1875** to curb skyrocketing inflation. This power play by Republicans prompted northerners to vote Democrat in the midterm elections of 1876, effectively ending Radical Reconstruction.

STRIKING DOWN RADICAL RECONSTRUCTION

By the mid-1870s, Democrats had retaken the South, reseating themselves in southern legislatures by driving blacks and white Unionists away from the polls and employing violence and other unethical tactics to win state elections. Most northerners looked the other way during this period, consumed by their own economic hardships.

In the late 1870s and early 1880s, a conservative Supreme Court also struck down much of the civil rights legislation that Radical Republicans had passed. In the 1873 **Slaughterhouse Cases**, the Court ruled that the Fourteenth Amendment safeguarded a person's rights only at a federal level, not at a state level (in rulings ten years later, the court further stipulated that the Fourteenth Amendment prohibited racial discrimination only by the U.S. government, not by individuals). In 1876, the Court ruled in *United States v. Cruikshank* that only states and their courts—not the federal government—could prosecute Ku Klux Klan members under the **Ku Klux Klan Act** of 1871.

The Disputed Election of 1876

As the election of 1876 approached, Democrats nominated **Samuel J. Tilden**, a lawyer famous for busting corrupt New York City politician **William "Boss" Tweed** in 1871. Tilden campaigned for restoration of the Union and an end to government corruption. The Republican Party, on the other hand, chose the virtually unknown **Rutherford B. Hayes**. Many Northern voters, tired of Reconstruction and hoping for more federal relief because of the depression, voted Democrat. Ultimately, Tilden received 250,000 more popular votes than Hayes, and 184 of the 185 electoral votes needed to become president.

The Compromise of 1877

With the election result hanging in the balance, Congress passed the **Electoral Count Act** in early 1877, creating a fifteen-man commission—eight Republicans and seven Democrats—to recount disputed votes in South Carolina, Louisiana, and Florida. Not surprisingly, the commission determined by an eight-to-seven vote that Republican Rutherford B. Hayes had carried all three states. Resentment and political deadlock threatened to divide the country, but both parties were able to avoid division and strike a deal with the **Compromise of 1877**. Democrats agreed to concede the presidency to the Republicans in exchange for the complete withdrawal of federal troops from the South. Hayes became president, withdrew the troops, and ended Reconstruction.

Key People & Terms

People

John Wilkes Booth
A well-known stage actor and fanatic supporter of the South who assassinated President **Abraham Lincoln** on April 14, 1865, during a performance at Ford's Theatre in Washington, D.C. After Lincoln's death, Vice President **Andrew Johnson** became president.

Ulysses S. Grant
Union general and Civil War hero who went on to defeat Horatio Seymour in the presidential election of 1868. Nicknamed "Unconditional Surrender" due to his hard-nosed war tactics, Grant joined the Republican Party and entered politics during the Reconstruction years. He served briefly as secretary of war after **Andrew Johnson** fired **Edwin M. Stanton** but resigned after Congress forced Johnson to reinstate Stanton. Although Grant himself was an honest man, his cabinet was corrupt, and numerous scandals, such as the **Fisk-Gould gold scheme**, **Crédit Mobilier**, and the **Whiskey Ring**, marred his presidency. He retired after his second term.

Horace Greeley
Former *New York Tribune* editor who ran for president in the election of 1872. The Democrats and **Liberal Republicans** both nominated Horace Greeley for president that year because they both desired limited government, reform, and a swift end to Reconstruction. This political alliance, however, ultimately weakened the Liberal Republicans' cause in the North, because most Americans still did not trust the Democratic Party. In the election, **Ulysses S. Grant** easily defeated Greeley.

Rutherford B. Hayes
Republican governor from Ohio and presidential nominee who ran against Democrat **Samuel J. Tilden** in the election of 1876. Republicans chose Hayes because he was virtually unknown in the political world, had no controversial opinions, and came from the politically important state of Ohio. In the wake of the scandals associated with **Ulysses S. Grant**'s presidency, Hayes's clean political record made him a sound candidate. Although Hayes received fewer popular and

electoral votes than Tilden in the election, he nonetheless became president after the **Compromise of 1877**.

ANDREW JOHNSON

Former governor and senator from Tennessee who became president after **Abraham Lincoln**'s assassination. Lincoln chose Johnson as his running mate in the 1864 election in order to persuade the conservative border states to remain in the Union. Johnson, neither a friend of the southern aristocracy nor a proponent of securing rights for former slaves, fought Congress over passage of the **Fourteenth Amendment** and the **Civil Rights Bill of 1866**. Johnson also believed that only he, not Congress, should be responsible for Reconstruction, recognizing new state governments according to the **Ten-Percent Plan** without Congress's consent. The House of Representatives **impeached** Johnson in 1868 for violating the **Tenure of Office Act**, but the Senate later acquitted him.

ABRAHAM LINCOLN

Former lawyer from Illinois who became president in the election of 1860 and guided the Union through the Civil War. In 1863, after several significant Union victories, Lincoln proposed the **Ten-Percent Plan** for Reconstruction of the South. He was unable to carry out the plan, however, because he was assassinated by **John Wilkes Booth** on April 14, 1865, at Ford's Theatre in Washington, D.C.

EDWIN M. STANTON

Secretary of war under **Abraham Lincoln** and **Andrew Johnson**. A former Democrat, Stanton joined the Republicans and went on to support **Radical Reconstruction** in the South. Johnson and Stanton butted heads on Reconstruction policy, however—so much so that **Radical Republicans** in Congress passed the **Tenure of Office Act** in 1867, requiring Johnson to seek Congress's permission before removing any congressionally appointed cabinet members. When Johnson ignored the act and fired Stanton, Republicans in the House countered by impeaching Johnson.

SAMUEL J. TILDEN

A former New York prosecutor who ran for president against **Rutherford B. Hayes** in 1876. Tilden first became famous in 1871 when he brought down New York City politician **William "Boss" Tweed** on corruption charges. Although Tilden received more popular votes than Hayes in the election of 1876, he fell one electoral vote shy of becoming president, leaving the election outcome disputed and unresolved. Ultimately, Democrats and Republicans reached the **Compromise of 1877**, which stipulated that the Democrats concede the presidency to Hayes in exchange for a complete withdrawal of federal troops from the southern states.

WILLIAM "BOSS" TWEED

A corrupt New York Democrat who was exposed in 1872 by prominent lawyer and future presidential candidate **Samuel J. Tilden**. "Boss" Tweed controlled most of New York City, promising improved public works to immigrants and the poor in exchange for their votes. Although Tweed was eventually prosecuted and died in prison, the **Tweed Ring** came to exemplify the widespread corruption and graft in northern politics during the Reconstruction era and the Gilded Age that followed.

TERMS

BLACK CODES

Laws that were passed across the South in response to the **Civil Rights Act of 1866**, restricting blacks' freedom of speech, freedom of assembly, and legal rights, and outlawing unemployment, loitering, vagrancy, and interracial marriages. The codes were one of many techniques that southern whites used to keep blacks effectively enslaved for decades after the abolition of slavery. Some black codes appeared as early as 1865.

CARPETBAGGERS

A nickname for northerners who moved to the South after the Civil War, named for their tendency to carry their possessions with them in large carpetbags. Though some carpetbaggers migrated to strike it rich, most did so to promote modernization, education, and civil rights for former slaves in the South. Some carpetbaggers had influential roles in the new Republican state legislatures, much to the dismay of white southerners.

CIVIL RIGHTS ACT OF 1866

A bill that guaranteed blacks the right to **sue**, serve on **juries**, testify as **witnesses** against whites, and enter into legal **contracts**. The act did not give blacks the right to vote, because most **Radical Republicans** in 1866 remained unconvinced that black suffrage was a necessity. When more Radicals were elected to Congress that autumn, however, they did consider making black suffrage a requirement for a state's readmission into the Union. The act eventually led to the **Fourteenth Amendment** to the Constitution.

CIVIL RIGHTS ACT OF 1875
A bill that forbade racial discrimination in all public places. The act was the **Radical Republicans**' last legislative effort to protect the civil liberties of former slaves. Democrats in the House opposed the bill from the outset and consequently made sure it remained largely ineffectual.

CIVIL RIGHTS CASES OF 1883
A series of Supreme Court cases that countered **Radical Republican** legislation passed during Reconstruction and severely restricted blacks' civil liberties. The Court ruled that the **Civil Rights Act of 1875** was unconstitutional, citing the fact that the Fourteenth Amendment prohibited racial discrimination by the U.S. government but not by individuals. The decision was used to justify racist policies in both the South and the North.

COMPROMISE OF 1877
A political agreement that made **Rutherford B. Hayes** president (rather than **Samuel J. Tilden**) in exchange for a complete withdrawal of federal troops from the South, effectively ending Reconstruction. When neither Hayes nor Tilden won enough electoral votes to become president, the election fell into dispute, and Congress passed the **Electoral Count Act** to recount popular votes in three contested states. The special counting committee determined by just one vote that Hayes had received more votes in the three states and was therefore the next president of the United States. Democrats accused the Republican-majority committee of bias, so the Compromise of 1877 was struck to resolve the political crisis.

CRÉDIT MOBILIER
A dummy construction company formed in the 1860s by corrupt Union Pacific Railroad officials who hired themselves as contractors at inflated rates to gain huge profits. The railroad executives also bribed dozens of congressmen and members of **Ulysses S. Grant**'s cabinet, including Vice President **Schuyler Colfax**. Eventually exposed in 1872, the affair forced many politicians to resign and became the worst scandal that occurred during Grant's presidency.

DEPRESSION OF 1873

An economic depression—caused by bad loans and overspeculation in railroads and manufacturing—that turned the North's attention away from Reconstruction. Poor whites and blacks were hit hardest, and unemployment soared as high as 15 percent. The depression helped southern Democrats in their quest to regain political prominence in the South and diminished the reelection prospects for Republican candidates, who advocated hard-money policies and little immediate economic relief. Indeed, Democrats swept the congressional elections of 1874 and regained the majority in the House of Representatives for the first time since 1856, effectively ending **Radical Reconstruction**.

FIFTEENTH AMENDMENT

A constitutional amendment, ratified in 1870, that gave all American men the right to vote, regardless of race or wealth. The amendment enfranchised blacks and poor landless whites who had never been able to vote. **Radical Republicans** required southern states to ratify the amendment in order to be readmitted into the Union. The amendment's ratification angered many **suffragettes** who were fighting for a woman's right to vote.

FIRST RECONSTRUCTION ACT

A bill, passed by **Radical Republicans** in Congress in 1867, that treated Southern states as divided territories. Sometimes called the Military Reconstruction Act or the Reconstruction Act, the First Reconstruction Act divided the South into five districts, each governed by martial law. It was the first of a series of harsher bills that the Radicals passed that year.

FOURTEENTH AMENDMENT

A constitutional amendment, drafted by **Radical Republicans** in 1866 and ratified in 1868, that ensured that the liberties guaranteed to blacks in the **Civil Rights Act of 1866** could not be taken away. Like the Civil Rights Act, the Fourteenth Amendment granted citizenship to all Americans regardless of race (except Native Americans, who did not gain full citizenship until the twentieth century). The amendment consequently reversed the Supreme Court's ***Dred Scott v. Sanford*** decision of 1857.

FREEDMEN'S BUREAU

A government agency established by Congress in 1865 to distribute food, supplies, and confiscated land to former slaves. Although the bureau's worth proved questionable because of corruption within the organization and external pressure from southern whites (including President **Andrew Johnson**), it successfully established schools for blacks throughout the South.

KU KLUX KLAN (KKK)

A secret society formed in Tennessee in 1866 to terrorize blacks. Racist whites formed the **KKK** as a violent reaction to Congress's passage of the **Civil Rights Act of 1866**. Within a few years, the Klan had numerous branches in every southern state. Klansmen donned white sheets and threatened, beat, and even killed "upstart" blacks. Congress finally passed the **Ku Klux Klan Act** in 1871 to curb Klan activity and restore order in the South.

KU KLUX KLAN ACT OF 1871

A congressional bill passed in response to widespread **Ku Klux Klan** violence throughout the South. The Klan had been intimidating, beating, and murdering blacks in every southern state since 1866, and many blacks, though newly enfranchised, avoided the polls out of fear for their lives. Although violence spiraled out of control by the late 1860s and early 1870s because state legislatures turned a blind eye, the Ku Klux Klan Act restored order in the South in time for the elections of 1872.

LIBERAL REPUBLICANS

A political party that was formed prior to the elections of 1872 by Republicans who disagreed with moderate and **Radical Republican** ideologies. The **Liberal Republicans** campaigned on a platform of government reform, reduced government spending, and anti-corruption measures. They also wanted to end military Reconstruction in the South and bring about a swift restoration of the Union.

MILITARY RECONSTRUCTION ACT

See **First Reconstruction Act.**

PRESIDENTIAL RECONSTRUCTION

President **Andrew Johnson**'s plan for Reconstruction, which lasted from 1865–1867. Johnson, a Democrat from Tennessee, allowed southern states to reenter the Union, but only after 10 percent of the voting population took loyalty oaths to the United States. Johnson's **Presidential Reconstruction** was similar to Lincoln's **Ten-Percent Plan**, though Johnson pardoned thousands of high-ranking Confederate officials. Johnson was also a critic of the **Freedmen's Bureau** and attempted to do away with the program. Presidential Reconstruction ended when **Radical Republicans** took control of Congress in 1867 in the wake of Johnson's **"Swing Around the Circle"** speeches.

PROCLAMATION OF AMNESTY AND RECONSTRUCTION

Abraham Lincoln's 1863 Reconstruction proposal to boost support for the war in the North and persuade the South to surrender. The proclamation outlined Lincoln's **Ten-Percent Plan,** which declared that secessionist states could be readmitted into the Union after 10 percent of voters swore their allegiance to the U.S. government.

RADICAL RECONSTRUCTION

The period from 1867–1877 when **Radical Republicans** controlled the House of Representatives and the Senate, advocating for civil liberties and enfranchisement for former slaves. The party, known for its harsh policies toward the secessionist South, passed progressive legislation like the **Civil Rights Act of 1866**, the **First** and **Second Reconstruction Acts**, the **Ku Klux Klan Act** of 1871, the **Civil Rights Act of 1875**, and the **Thirteenth, Fourteenth,** and **Fifteenth Amendments**.

RADICAL REPUBLICANS

A Reconstruction-era political party known for its progressive legislation and harsh policies toward the South. The Radical Republicans passed the **Civil Rights Act of 1866**, the **First Reconstruction Act,** the **Second Reconstruction Act,** the **Ku Klux Klan Act** of 1871, the **Civil Rights Act of 1875,** and the **Thirteenth, Fourteenth,** and **Fifteenth Amendments**. Radical Republicans in the House also impeached President **Andrew Johnson** in 1868 but were unable to secure enough votes for a conviction in the Senate.

RECONSTRUCTION ACT

See **First Reconstruction Act.**

RESUMPTION ACT

An act that was passed in 1875 to reduce the amount of currency circulating in the economy during the **Depression of 1873**. Although the Resumption Act proved beneficial in the long run, its short-term effects on many Americans were detrimental. Democrats used these hard times to gain votes: **Samuel J. Tilden** ended up receiving more popular votes than **Rutherford B. Hayes** in the disputed election of 1876.

SCALAWAGS

White Unionist Republicans in the South who participated in efforts to modernize and transform the region after the Civil War. Though many **scalawags** had influential roles in the new state governments, southern whites deemed them traitors.

SECOND RECONSTRUCTION ACT
An act passed by Radical Republicans in 1867 that put federal troops in charge of voter registration in the South.

SHARECROPPING
An agricultural production system in the South through which wealthy landowners leased individual plots of land on plantations to white and black **sharecroppers** in exchange for a percentage of the yearly yield of crops. Blacks preferred this system to **wage labor** because it gave them a sense of independence and responsibility. Ironically, though, sharecroppers had less autonomy than wage laborers, because high debts bound them to the land, and most former slaves worked on plots owned by their former masters. By 1880, most southern blacks had become sharecroppers.

SLAUGHTERHOUSE CASES
A series of Supreme Court cases (involving a New Orleans slaughterhouse) that effectively rendered the **Fourteenth Amendment** useless. The justices ruled that the amendment protected citizens from rights infringements only on a federal level, not on a state level. This decision allowed state legislatures to suspend blacks' legal and civil rights as outlined in the Constitution.

"SWING AROUND THE CIRCLE"
The name for a group of speeches in which President **Andrew Johnson** blamed **Radical Republicans** for the slowness of Reconstruction and race riots in the South after the passage of the **Civil Rights Act of 1866**. Johnson traveled across the country, speaking out against Republicans, pro-war Democrats, blacks, and anyone else who challenged him. Consequently, his often-abrasive speeches further tarnished the Democratic Party's already scarred reputation and persuaded many northerners to vote Republican in the congressional elections of 1866.

TEN-PERCENT PLAN
Abraham Lincoln's plan for Reconstruction, under which secessionist states could be readmitted to the Union only after 10 percent of their voting population took a loyalty oath to the Union. Lincoln agreed to pardon most Confederates but made no provision for safeguarding the rights of former slaves. Many **Radical Republicans** believed his plan was too lenient.

TENURE OF OFFICE ACT

A bill that Congress passed during **Andrew Johnson**'s presidency that required Johnson to consult Congress before dismissing any congressionally appointed government official. When Johnson ignored Congress and fired Secretary of War **Edwin M. Stanton**, the **Radical Republicans** in the House impeached Johnson on the grounds that he had violated the Tenure of Office Act. Although Johnson technically *did* violate the act, the Radicals impeached him primarily out of revenge, angry that he had excluded Congress from the Reconstruction process. The Senate later acquitted Johnson, so he was not removed from office.

THIRTEENTH AMENDMENT

A constitutional amendment, ratified in 1865, that abolished slavery in the United States. Southern states were required to acknowledge and ratify the amendment before they were readmitted to the Union.

UNITED STATES V. CRUIKSHANK

An 1876 Supreme Court case that severely restricted Congress's ability to enforce the **Ku Klux Klan Act** of 1871. The Court ruled that only states, not the U.S. government, had the right to prosecute Klansmen under the law. Without the threat of federal prosecution, the **Ku Klux Klan** and other racist whites had free reign to terrorize blacks throughout the South.

WADE-DAVIS BILL

An 1864 bill that stipulated that southern states could reenter the Union only after 50 percent of their voters pledged allegiance to the United States. **Radical Republicans** passed the bill in response to **Abraham Lincoln**'s **Ten-Percent Plan**, which they believed was too lenient. Lincoln ultimately **pocket-vetoed** the bill, so it did not come into effect. The Wade-Davis Bill was the first of many clashes between the White House and Congress for control over the Reconstruction process.

WHISKEY RING

A group of government officials who embezzled millions of dollars of excise tax revenue from the U.S. Treasury. The **Whiskey Ring scandal** damaged President **Ulysses S. Grant**'s reputation and affected central figures in the White House—the president's own personal secretary was indicted in the conspiracy but was acquitted after Grant testified to his innocence.

Summary & Analysis

Lincoln's Ten-Percent Plan: 1863–1865

EVENTS

1863 Lincoln issues Proclamation of Amnesty and Reconstruction

1864 Congress passes Wade-Davis Bill; Lincoln pocket-vetoes it

1865 Lee surrenders to Grant at Appomattox Courthouse
      Congress creates Freedmen's Bureau
      Lincoln is assassinated; Johnson becomes president

KEY PEOPLE

Abraham Lincoln 16th U.S. president; proposed Ten-Percent Plan for Reconstruction in
      1863; assassinated by John Wilkes Booth in 1865
Andrew Johnson 17th U.S. president; was vice president in Lincoln's second term and
      became president upon Lincoln's assassination

PLANS FOR RECONSTRUCTION

After major Union victories at the battles of Gettysburg and Vicksburg in 1863, President **Abraham Lincoln** began preparing his plan for **Reconstruction** to reunify the North and South after the war's end. Because Lincoln believed that the South had never legally seceded from the Union, his plan for Reconstruction was based on forgiveness. He thus issued the **Proclamation of Amnesty and Reconstruction** in 1863 to announce his intention to reunite the once-united states. Lincoln hoped that the proclamation would rally northern support for the war and persuade weary Confederate soldiers to surrender.

THE TEN-PERCENT PLAN

Lincoln's blueprint for Reconstruction included the **Ten-Percent Plan,** which specified that a southern state could be readmitted into the Union once 10 percent of its voters (from the voter rolls for the election of 1860) swore an **oath of allegiance** to the Union. Voters could then elect delegates to draft revised state constitutions and establish new state governments. All southerners except for high-ranking Confederate army officers and government officials would be granted a full pardon. Lincoln guaranteed southerners that he would protect their private property, though not their slaves. Most moderate Republicans in Congress supported the president's proposal for Reconstruction because they wanted to bring a quick end to the war.

In many ways, the Ten-Percent Plan was more of a political maneuver than a plan for Reconstruction. Lincoln wanted to end the war quickly. He feared that a protracted war would lose public support and that the North and South would never be reunited if the fighting did not stop quickly. His fears were justified: by late 1863, a large number of Democrats were clamoring for a truce and peaceful resolution. Lincoln's Ten-Percent Plan was thus lenient—an attempt to entice the South to surrender.

Lincoln's Vision for Reconstruction

President Lincoln seemed to favor self-Reconstruction by the states with little assistance from Washington. To appeal to poorer whites, he offered to **pardon** all Confederates; to appeal to former plantation owners and southern aristocrats, he pledged to **protect private property**. Unlike **Radical Republicans** in Congress, Lincoln did not want to punish southerners or reorganize southern society. His actions indicate that he wanted Reconstruction to be a short process in which secessionist states could draft new constitutions as swiftly as possible so that the United States could exist as it had before. But historians can only speculate that Lincoln desired a swift reunification, for his assassination in 1865 cut his plans for Reconstruction short.

Louisiana Drafts a New Constitution

White southerners in the Union-occupied state of **Louisiana** met in 1864—before the end of the Civil War—to draft a new constitution in accordance with the Ten-Percent Plan. The progressive delegates promised free public schooling, improvements to the labor system, and public works projects. They also abolished slavery in the state but refused to give the would-be freed slaves the right to vote. Although Lincoln approved of the new constitution, Congress rejected it and refused to acknowledge the state delegates who won in Louisiana in the election of 1864.

The Radical Republicans

Many leading Republicans in Congress feared that Lincoln's plan for Reconstruction was not harsh enough, believing that the South needed to be punished for causing the war. These **Radical Republicans** hoped to control the Reconstruction process, transform southern society, disband the planter aristocracy, redistribute land, develop industry, and guarantee civil liberties for former slaves. Although the Radical Republicans were the minority party in Congress, they managed to sway many moderates in the postwar years and came to dominate Congress in later sessions.

THE WADE-DAVIS BILL

In the summer of 1864, the Radical Republicans passed the **Wade-Davis Bill** to counter Lincoln's Ten-Percent Plan. The bill stated that a southern state could rejoin the Union only if 50 percent of its registered voters swore an "ironclad oath" of allegiance to the United States. The bill also established safeguards for black civil liberties but did not give blacks the right to vote.

President Lincoln feared that asking 50 percent of voters to take a loyalty oath would ruin any chance of ending the war swiftly. Moreover, 1864 was an election year, and he could not afford to have northern voters see him as an uncompromising radical. Because the Wade-Davis Bill was passed near the end of Congress's session, Lincoln was able to **pocket-veto** it, effectively blocking the bill by refusing to sign it before Congress went into recess.

THE FREEDMEN'S BUREAU

The president and Congress disagreed not only about the best way to readmit southern states to the Union but also about the best way to redistribute southern land. Lincoln, for his part, authorized several of his wartime generals to resettle former slaves on confiscated lands. General William Tecumseh Sherman's **Special Field Order No. 15** set aside land in South Carolina and islands off the coast of Georgia for roughly 40,000 former slaves. Congress, meanwhile, created the **Freedmen's Bureau** in early 1865 to distribute food and supplies, establish schools, and redistribute additional confiscated land to former slaves and poor whites. Anyone who pledged loyalty to the Union could lease **forty acres** of land from the bureau and then have the option to purchase them several years later.

EFFECTIVENESS OF THE FREEDMEN'S BUREAU

The Freedmen's Bureau was only slightly more successful than the pocket-vetoed Wade-Davis Bill. Most southerners regarded the bureau as a nuisance and a threat to their way of life during the postwar depression. The southern aristocracy saw the bureau as a northern attempt to redistribute their lands to former slaves and resisted the Freedmen's Bureau from its inception. Plantation owners threatened their former slaves into selling their forty acres of land, and many bureau agents accepted bribes, turning a blind eye to abuses by former slave owners. Despite these failings, however, the Freedman's Bureau did succeed in setting up schools in the South for nearly 250,000 free blacks.

LINCOLN'S ASSASSINATION

At the end of the Civil War, in the spring of 1865, Lincoln and Congress were on the brink of a political showdown with their competing plans for Reconstruction. But on April 14, **John Wilkes Booth**, a popular stage actor from Maryland who was sympathetic to the secessionist South, shot Lincoln at Ford's Theatre in Washington, D.C. When Lincoln died the following day, Vice President **Andrew Johnson**, a Democrat from Tennessee, became president.

SUMMARY & ANALYSIS

PRESIDENTIAL RECONSTRUCTION: 1865–1867

EVENTS

1865	Lincoln is assassinated; Johnson becomes president
	Congress establishes Joint Committee on Reconstruction
1866	Johnson vetoes renewal of Freedmen's Bureau charter
	Congress passes Civil Rights Act of 1866 over Johnson's veto
	Congress drafts Fourteenth Amendment
	Johnson delivers "Swing Around the Circle" speeches

KEY PEOPLE

Andrew Johnson 17th U.S. president; fought Radical Republicans in Congress over key Reconstruction legislation

RECONSTRUCTION AFTER LINCOLN

Lincoln's assassination seemingly gave **Radical Republicans** in Congress the clear path they needed to implement their plan for Reconstruction. The new president, **Andrew Johnson**, had seemed supportive of punitive measures against the South in the past: he disliked the southern planter elite and believed they had been a major cause of the Civil War. But Johnson surprised Radical Republicans by consistently blocking their attempts to pass punitive legislation.

JOHNSON, LAISSEZ-FAIRE, AND STATES' RIGHTS

Johnson, a Democrat, preferred a stronger state government (in relation to the federal government) and believed in the doctrine of *laissez-faire*, which stated that the federal government should stay out of the economic and social affairs of its people. Even after the Civil War, Johnson believed that **states' rights** took precedence over central authority, and he disapproved of legislation that affected the American economy. He rejected all Radical Republican attempts to dissolve the plantation system, reorganize the southern economy, and protect the civil rights of blacks.

Although Johnson disliked the southern planter elite, his actions suggest otherwise: he pardoned more people than any president before him, and most of those pardoned were wealthy southern landowners. Johnson also shared southern aristocrats' racist point of view that former slaves should not receive the same rights as whites in the Union. Johnson opposed the **Freedmen's Bureau** because he felt that targeting former slaves for special assistance would be detrimental to the South. He also believed the bureau was an example of the federal government assuming political power reserved to the states, which went against his pro–states' rights ideology.

PRESIDENTIAL RECONSTRUCTION

Like Lincoln, Johnson wanted to restore the Union in as little time as possible. While Congress was in recess, the president began implementing his plans, which became known as **Presidential Reconstruction.** He returned confiscated property to white southerners, issued hundreds of pardons to former Confederate officers and government officials, and undermined the Freedmen's Bureau by ordering it to return all confiscated lands to white landowners. Johnson also appointed governors to supervise the drafting of new state constitutions and agreed to readmit each state provided it ratified the **Thirteenth Amendment**, which abolished slavery. Hoping that Reconstruction would be complete by the time Congress reconvened a few months later, he declared Reconstruction over at the end of 1865.

THE JOINT COMMITTEE ON RECONSTRUCTION

Radical and moderate Republicans in Congress were furious that Johnson had organized his own Reconstruction efforts in the South without their consent. Johnson did not offer any security for former slaves, and his pardons allowed many of the same wealthy southern landowners who had held power before the war to regain control of the state governments. To challenge Presidential Reconstruction, Congress established the **Joint Committee on Reconstruction** in late 1865, and the committee began to devise stricter requirements for readmitting southern states.

THE END OF THE FREEDMEN'S BUREAU

Early in 1866, Congress voted to renew the charter that had created the **Freedmen's Bureau,** in retaliation for the fact that Johnson had stripped the bureau of its power. Congress also revised the charter to include special legal courts that would override southern courts. Johnson, however, **vetoed** the renewed Freedmen's Bureau, once again using the states' rights argument that the federal government should not deprive the states of their judicial powers. Johnson also claimed that it was not the federal government's responsibility to provide special protection for blacks. Although Congress's first attempt to override the veto failed, a second attempt succeeded in preserving the bureau. The bureau was weakened, however, and Congress finally terminated it in 1872.

THE CIVIL RIGHTS ACT OF 1866

A few months after the battle over the Freedmen's Bureau charter, Congress passed the **Civil Rights Act of 1866**. The act guaranteed citizenship to all Americans regardless of race (except, in an unfortunate irony, Native Americans) and secured former slaves the right to own property, sue, testify in court, and sign legal contracts. President Johnson vetoed this bill as well, but Radical Republicans managed to secure enough votes to override it.

THE FOURTEENTH AMENDMENT

Shortly after passing the Civil Rights Act of 1866, Congress drafted the **Fourteenth Amendment** to the U.S. Constitution to ensure that the 1866 act would have its intended power. Although the amendment did not give former slaves the right to vote, it guaranteed citizenship to all males born in the United States, regardless of race. Republicans in Congress specified that southern states had to ratify the amendment before they could reenter the Union. In 1868, enough states ratified, and the Fourteenth Amendment was added to the Constitution.

PROTECTIONS FOR FORMER SLAVES

The Civil Rights Act of 1866 and the Fourteenth Amendment were milestones in the fight to give former slaves equal rights. The Civil Rights Act was the first piece of congressional legislation to override state laws and protect civil liberties. More important, it reversed the 1857 *Dred Scott v. Sanford* ruling by the U.S. Supreme Court, which stated that blacks were not citizens, effectively legalizing slavery. In giving former slaves citizenship, the Civil Rights Act also gave them—at least in theory—equal protection under the law.

The ratification of the Fourteenth Amendment guaranteed that from that point onward, no one in the United States—even a Supreme Court justice or president—could deny a black person citizenship rights on the basis of racial inequality. Constitutional law stood in the way. Of course, *true* equality did not happen in a day; the first real steps would not be taken for another hundred years. But the Fourteenth Amendment was a significant start.

JOHNSON'S "SWING AROUND THE CIRCLE"

Many southern whites were angered by the Civil Rights Act of 1866 and the Fourteenth Amendment. Angry mobs took to the streets in communities throughout the South, and riots erupted in Memphis and New Orleans, leaving many innocent blacks dead. The violence shocked many northerners, who accused President Johnson of turning a blind eye. The president, in turn, placed the blame on Radical Republicans in Congress during his infamous **"Swing Around the**

Circle," in which he traveled throughout the country giving speeches that lambasted Republicans, pro-war Democrats, and blacks. Rather than drum up support, however, Johnson's coarse rhetoric hurt the Democratic Party's credibility and persuaded many northerners to vote Republican in the congressional elections of 1866.

THE NORTHERN RESPONSE

Ironically, the southern race riots and Johnson's "Swing Around the Circle" tour convinced northerners that Congress was *not* being harsh enough toward the postwar South. Many northerners were troubled by the presidential pardons Johnson had handed out to Confederates, his decision to strip the Freedmen's Bureau of its power, and the fact that blacks were essentially slaves again on white plantations. Moreover, many in the North believed that a president sympathetic to southern racists and secessionists could not properly reconstruct the South. As a result, Radical Republicans overwhelmingly beat their Democratic opponents in the elections of 1866, ending Presidential Reconstruction and ushering in the era of **Radical Reconstruction.**

SUMMARY & ANALYSIS

Radical Reconstruction: 1867–1877

Events

1867	Congress passes First and Second Reconstruction Acts Congress passes Tenure of Office Act
1868	House of Representatives impeaches Andrew Johnson Senate acquits Johnson Fourteenth Amendment is ratified Ulysses S. Grant is elected president
1870	Fifteenth Amendment is ratified

Key People

Andrew Johnson 17th U.S. president; impeached by the House of Representatives in 1868 but later acquitted by the Senate

Edwin M. Stanton Secretary of War under Lincoln and Johnson; was dismissed by Johnson, prompting House Republicans to impeach Johnson

Ulysses S. Grant 18th U.S. president; formerly a Union general and, briefly, secretary of war under Johnson

Radical Reconstruction

After sweeping the elections of 1866, the **Radical Republicans** gained almost complete control over policymaking in Congress. Along with their more moderate Republican allies, they gained control of the House of Representatives and the Senate and thus gained sufficient power to override any potential vetoes by President **Andrew Johnson**. This political ascension, which occurred in early 1867, marked the beginning of **Radical Reconstruction** (also known as **Congressional Reconstruction**).

The First and Second Reconstruction Acts

Congress began the task of Reconstruction by passing the **First Reconstruction Act** in March 1867. Also known as the **Military Reconstruction Act** or simply the **Reconstruction Act**, the bill reduced the secessionist states to little more than conquered territory, dividing them into five **military districts**, each governed by a Union general. Congress declared **martial law** in the territories, dispatching troops to keep the peace and protect former slaves.

Congress also declared that southern states needed to redraft their constitutions, ratify the **Fourteenth Amendment**, and provide suffrage to blacks in order to seek readmission into the Union. To further safeguard voting rights for former slaves, Republicans passed the **Second Reconstruction Act**, placing Union troops in charge of voter registration. Congress overrode two presidential vetoes from Johnson to pass the bills.

REESTABLISHING ORDER IN THE SOUTH

The murderous **Memphis and New Orleans race riots** of 1866 proved that Reconstruction needed to be declared *and* enforced, and the Military Reconstruction Act jump-started this process. Congress chose to send the military, creating "radical regimes" throughout the secessionist states. Radical Republicans hoped that by declaring martial law in the South and passing the Second Reconstruction Act, they would be able to create a Republican political base in the seceded states to facilitate their plans for Radical Reconstruction. Though most southern whites hated the "regimes" that Congress established, they proved successful in speeding up Reconstruction. Indeed, by 1870 all of the southern states had been readmitted to the Union.

RADICAL RECONSTRUCTION'S EFFECT ON BLACKS

Though Radical Reconstruction was an improvement on President Johnson's *laissez-faire* Reconstructionism, it had its ups and downs. The daily lives of blacks and poor whites changed little. While Radicals in Congress successfully passed rights legislation, southerners all but ignored these laws. The newly formed southern governments established public schools, but they were still segregated and did not receive enough funding. Black literacy rates did improve, but marginally at best.

THE TENURE OF OFFICE ACT

In addition to the Reconstruction Acts, Congress also passed a series of bills in 1867 to limit President Johnson's power, one of which was the **Tenure of Office Act**. The bill sought to protect prominent Republicans in the Johnson administration by forbidding their removal without congressional consent. Although the act applied to all officeholders whose appointment required congressional approval, Republicans were specifically aiming to keep Secretary of War **Edwin M. Stanton** in office, because Stanton was the Republicans' conduit for controlling the U.S. military. Defiantly, Johnson ignored the act, fired Stanton in the summer of 1867 (while Congress was in recess), and replaced him with Union general **Ulysses S. Grant**. Afraid that Johnson would end Military Reconstruction in the South, Congress ordered him to reinstate Stanton when it reconvened in 1868. Johnson refused, but Grant resigned, and Congress put Edwin M. Stanton back in office over the president's objections.

JOHNSON'S IMPEACHMENT

House Republicans, tired of presidential vetoes that blocked Military Reconstruction, **impeached** Johnson by a vote of 126–47 for violating the Tenure of Office Act. The Senate then tried Johnson in May 1868 in front of a gallery of spectators. However, the prosecutors, two Radical Republicans from the House, were unable to convince a majority of senators to convict the president. Seven Republican senators sided with Senate Democrats, and the Republicans fell one vote shy of convicting Johnson.

THE POLITICS OF JOHNSON'S IMPEACHMENT

Although Johnson did technically violate the **Tenure of Office Act**, the bill was passed primarily as a means to provoke Johnson and give Radical Republicans in Congress an excuse to get rid of him. Indeed, Johnson's trial in Congress exposed the real reason that House Republicans impeached the president: he had ignored them in the process of crafting Reconstruction policies, and they wanted retaliation.

The Senate, however, acquitted Johnson, aware that a frivolous impeachment would have set a dangerous precedent. If Congress had removed a president from office simply on the basis of a power struggle between the president and Congress, they might have endangered the system of separation of powers—an integral part of U.S. government. Although Johnson had stubbornly opposed Congress, he had not violated the Constitution and was not guilty of committing "high crimes and misdemeanors."

In addition, another factor was the fact that, because Johnson had no vice president, the president *pro tempore* of the Senate was next in line for the presidency should Johnson be impeached. This man was a rather liberal Republican named Benjamin Wade, whose politics did not sit well with certain other senate Republicans. Some of these Republicans deemed the prospect of a Wade presidency just as unpalatable as the dangerous precedent of impeachment and thus voted with the Democrats to acquit Johnson.

THE FIFTEENTH AMENDMENT

The **Thirteenth** and **Fourteenth Amendments** had abolished slavery and granted blacks citizenship, but blacks still did not have the right to vote. Radical Republicans feared that black suffrage might be revoked in the future, so they decided to amend the Constitution to solidify this right. They also believed that giving blacks the right to vote would weaken southern elites, who had regained political power in the South. In 1869, therefore, Congress passed the **Fifteenth**

Amendment, granting all American males the right to vote. Congress also required secessionist states that had not yet reentered the Union to ratify the amendment in order to rejoin. By 1870, three-quarters of the Union had ratified the amendment, and it became law.

BLACK VOTERS

After the amendment's ratification, southern blacks flocked to the polls. By the beginning of 1868, more than 700,000 blacks (and nearly the same number of poor landless whites) had registered to vote. Not surprisingly, virtually all of them declared themselves **Republicans**, associating the Democratic Party with secession and slavery. Black civic societies and grassroots political organizations began to sprout up across the South, most led by prominent blacks who had been freedmen since before the Civil War.

Soon, black voters gained majorities in South Carolina, Alabama, Louisiana, Florida, and Mississippi and were able to facilitate Republican plans for Reconstruction. These voters elected many **black politicians** in the majority states and throughout the South: fourteen black politicians were elected to the U.S. House of Representatives, and two to the Mississippi State Senate. These new state governments funded the creation of roads, hospitals, prisons, and free public schools.

THE FIFTEENTH AMENDMENT IN PERSPECTIVE

Prior to 1866, most Republicans had opposed black suffrage. Even the "Great Emancipator" himself, Abraham Lincoln, considered giving the right to vote only to blacks who were freedmen before the Civil War and those who had served in the Union Army. Most moderate Republicans saw freedmen suffrage as unnecessary until they realized that the Republican Party would never gain influence in the South unless blacks had the right to vote. Blacks would support the Republican Party en masse, so ratifying the Fifteenth Amendment guaranteed Republicans this support.

Ironically, the Fifteenth Amendment also forced reluctant *northern* states to give blacks the right to vote. Even though most of the new postwar state constitutions in the South gave blacks the right to vote, many northern states refused to follow suit, because they considered universal manhood suffrage a solution unique to the South that was unnecessary in the North.

The amendment also granted voting rights to poor whites, especially in the South. Prior to the Civil War, landowners were the only social group who had the privilege to vote, excluding the majority of poor, landless whites from active political participation. The Fifteenth Amendment thus brought sweeping changes for blacks, poor whites, and politics in general in the United States.

REACTION FROM SUFFRAGETTES

The Fifteenth Amendment did not secure the right to vote for all Americans: women still did not have the right to vote, and leaders in the **women's suffrage** movement felt betrayed by their exclusion from the amendment. Prior to the Civil War, the women's suffrage movement and the **abolition movement** had been closely related: both groups strived to achieve political and civil rights for the underrepresented in society.

After the Union victory, prominent women in the movement, such as **Elizabeth Cady Stanton** and **Susan B. Anthony**, saw a window of opportunity: they believed that with progressive, Unionist support in Congress, blacks and women would achieve enfranchisement. Radical Republicans in Congress believed otherwise. Republicans assumed that if Congress granted all men *and* women the right to vote, their party would lose support in both the South and North. As it turned out, women would have to wait almost fifty more years for the passage of the Nineteenth Amendment that granted them the right to vote.

THE POSTWAR SOUTH AND THE BLACK CODES: 1865–1877

EVENTS

1865	Southern states begin to issue black codes
1866	Congress passes Civil Rights Act of 1866 Ku Klux Klan forms
1867	Radical Reconstruction begins Congress passes First Reconstruction Act
1868	Fourteenth Amendment is ratified
1870	Fifteenth Amendment is ratified
1871	Congress passes Ku Klux Klan Act of 1871

THE SOUTH AFTER THE WAR

While politicians in Washington, D.C., were busy passing Recon-struction legislation in the late 1860s, the South remained in upheaval, as the ruined economy tried to accommodate newly emancipated blacks and political power struggles ensued. As freed slaves tried to establish livelihoods for themselves and take advan-tage of their new rights under the Fourteenth and Fifteenth Amend-ments, politicians and vigilantes used insidious legislation and intimidation to try to maintain the prewar status quo.

NEWLY EMANCIPATED BLACKS

The Union Army's advance deep into southern territory in the final months of the Civil War freed thousands and thousands of slaves. Although some of these slaves were emancipated officially in the final days of the conflict, most freed themselves, simply refusing to work or walking away from the fields to follow the Union Army.

The end of the war meant that thousands of blacks could search freely for family members from whom they had been separated when they were sold or auctioned. Many black couples took the opportunity to get married after being freed, knowing that they could never again be lawfully separated. The number of black mar-riages skyrocketed.

BLACK SCHOOLS AND CHURCHES

Many freed blacks, previously forbidden to learn to read or write, wanted their children to receive the education that they themselves had been denied. The Congress-created **Freedmen's Bureau**, assisted by former abolitionist organizations in the North, succeeded in establishing schools for thousands of blacks during the late 1860s.

In addition, many former slaves established their own **churches**. White southern clergymen had often defended slavery in their sermons in the period before the Civil War. As a result, blacks distrusted their white congregations, so they created their own as soon as they had the opportunity.

Carpetbaggers and Scalawags

Meanwhile, some northerners jumped at the opportunity to move to the South in the wake of the Confederacy's defeat. Commonly known as **carpetbaggers** because of their tendency to carry their possessions in large carpetbags, some moved from the North to promote education, others to modernize the South, and others to seek their fortune. White southern Unionists, or **scalawags**, attempted to achieve similar aims. Carpetbaggers and scalawags served in state legislatures in every southern state during Reconstruction.

Sharecropping

Despite efforts by white landowners to force blacks back into wage labor on large plantations, emancipation enabled southern blacks to rent their own plots of land, farm them, and provide for their families. A system of **sharecropping** emerged in which many former plantation owners divided their lands and rented out each plot, or **share**, to a black family. The family farmed their own crops and rented their plot of land in exchange for a percentage of their crop's yield. Some poor, landless whites also became sharecroppers, farming lands owned by wealthy planter elites. By 1880, the vast majority of farmers in the South were sharecroppers.

Unfortunately, the economic prospects for blacks under the sharecropping system were usually poor. Many former slaves ended up sharecropping on land owned by their former masters, and the system kept blacks tied to their shares—their rented plots of land—and thereby indebted to white landowners. Moreover, because cotton prices dropped steadily from about fifty cents per pound in 1864 to a little over ten cents per pound by the end of Reconstruction, sharecroppers' incomes were meager. Most black farmers were able to purchase items only on credit at local shops—almost always owned by their landlords—and thus went deep into debt.

The Black Codes

Despite the efforts of Radical Republicans in Congress, the white elite in the South did everything it could to prevent blacks from gaining civic power. In reaction to the **Civil Rights Act** of 1866, every southern legislature passed laws to restrict opportunities for blacks. These **black codes**, which ranged widely in severity, outlawed everything from interracial marriage to loitering in public areas. One code outlawed unemployment, which allowed white landowners to threaten their tenant farmers with eviction if they decided to give up their land. The black codes in Mississippi were arguably the worst: they stripped blacks of their right to serve on juries and testify against whites, and also outlawed free speech. Other codes forced black children into unpaid apprenticeships that usually led to fieldwork.

Southern whites passed these laws because they feared black political influence, especially in states like South Carolina where blacks outnumbered whites. Many racist white southerners also worried that freed slaves would seek revenge on their masters, rape white women, and ruin the economy. Wealthy southern landowners, for their part, supported the black codes because the codes ensured that they would have a stable and reliable black workforce. Some of the black codes forced former slaves to sign contracts, requiring them to work for meager wages, while some even required them to work on chain gangs in the fields.

Once the Republican Party took control of Reconstruction, they forced southern state legislatures to repeal many of the black codes. Nonetheless, many wealthy white southerners continued to enforce the codes unlawfully for years, even decades, after Reconstruction.

THE KU KLUX KLAN

Despite the progress blacks made in the South after the Fourteenth and Fifteenth Amendments, racism still existed, and angry whites sometimes resorted to violence to intimidate blacks. The most notorious of these initiatives was the **Ku Klux Klan**, a secret society of white supremacists formed in Tennessee in 1866 to terrorize blacks. Klansmen, who wore white hoods to conceal their identities, harassed and beat blacks, carpetbaggers, and scalawags, and sometimes even conducted **lynchings**—mob killings of blacks, usually by hanging.

The Klan often used these tactics to scare blacks away from the polls during elections and to punish those who did not obey their demands. In one extreme case, Klansmen murdered several hundred black voters in Louisiana in 1868. Congress, realizing the need to protect blacks, passed the **Ku Klux Klan Act** of 1871 to try to curb the tide of violence and intimidation.

Grant's Presidency: 1869–1876

Events

1868	Ulysses S. Grant is elected president
1869	Fisk-Gould Gold scheme evolves
1871	Tweed Ring is exposed
1872	Liberal Republican Party emerges Grant is reelected Crédit Mobilier scandal is exposed
1873	Depression of 1873 hits
1874	Whiskey Ring scandal occurs
1875	Congress passes Resumption Act

Key People

Ulysses S. Grant 18th U.S. president; served two terms marred by corruption and scandal

Horatio Seymour Former governor of New York; 1868 Democratic presidential nominee

William "Boss" Tweed Corrupt Democratic politician from New York who took advantage of immigrants and the poor, promising improved public works in exchange for votes

Samuel J. Tilden Famous New York prosecutor who brought down "Boss" Tweed in 1871 on corruption charges; later ran for president in 1876

Horace Greeley Former *New York Tribune* editor; Democratic and Liberal Republican nominee for president in 1872

The Election of 1868

As the presidential election of 1868 drew near, Republicans nominated Civil War hero **Ulysses S. Grant**. Although Grant had never held public office, he had been a successful Union general, was popular in the North, and served as a reminder that Republicans had won the war. Democrats nominated **Horatio Seymour**, a former governor of New York who opposed emancipation, supported states' rights, and wanted to regain control of Reconstruction from Congress. Although Grant received 214 electoral votes to Seymour's 80, he won the popular vote by only 300,000, a slim margin. Republicans maintained control of Congress.

The Start of the Gilded Age

Grant's presidency marked the beginning of the **Gilded Age**—the name that novelist Mark Twain gave to the postwar, post-Reconstruction era of big business, graft, and scandal that lasted until about 1900. The Gilded Age was enabled partly because most presidents during this era, including Grant, were weak in relation to Congress. The U.S. government's economic policy became lax during these years, allowing

Americans to take advantage of the *laissez-faire* economics via increased speculation, investment, and corruption.

THE FISK-GOULD GOLD SCHEME

Indeed, Grant had not even completed his first year in office before scandal hit. In 1869, financial tycoons **Jim Fisk** and **Jay Gould** bribed officials in Grant's cabinet, including Grant's own brother-in-law, to turn a blind eye while the two wealthy businessmen attempted to corner the gold market. Fisk and Gould even conned Grant himself into not releasing any more of the precious metal into the economy.

Fisk and Gould's attempt to corner the gold market led to the panic of September 24, 1869, **"Black Friday."** Congress was able to restore gold prices only after releasing more gold into the economy, despite Grant's promise that more gold would not be released. Though Grant was unknowingly part of the scandal, no formal charges were filed against him.

THE TWEED RING

Historians also associate the Grant presidency with corrupt political bosses and **"machines,"** the most notorious of which was the **Tammany Hall** machine in New York City, led by **William "Boss" Tweed**. Tweed, more than anyone else, was the symbol of corruption during the Gilded Age: he controlled nearly every aspect of political life in New York City; used bribery, extortion, and fraud to get what he wanted; and even sponsored phony elections to put his associates in office. Historians estimate that he may have fleeced as much as $200 million from New Yorkers. Though it could be argued that Tweed preyed on recent immigrants, he also provided valuable services for them: Tammany Hall often gave newly arrived immigrants housing, jobs, and security in exchange for votes.

The law finally caught up with Tweed in 1871, when New York prosecutor **Samuel J. Tilden** helped expose the Democratic politician's corrupt dealings and sent him to jail. Tweed ultimately died in prison. Tilden, for his part, capitalized on his sudden fame and entered politics; within five years, he ran for president of the United States.

EMERGENCE OF THE RAILROADS

Grant's presidency also saw a flurry of **railroad** construction throughout the United States, meaning big business for railroaders both North and South. American industrial production was booming (mostly in the North), and the demand for railroad lines to transport manufactured goods throughout the country had rapidly increased. During the Civil War, the U.S. government had granted subsidies to large railroad companies like the **Union Pacific Railroad** and the **Central Pacific Railroad** to lay rail tracks throughout the North and West. In 1869, these northern and western railroad systems were finally united when Union Pacific and Central Pacific lines were joined at **Promontory**, Utah, forming a transcontinental rail link.

THE CRÉDIT MOBILIER SCANDAL
This booming railroad industry quickly attracted corporate corruption. In the 1860s, corrupt Union Pacific Railroad executives had created a dummy railroad construction company called **Crédit Mobilier**. The executives contracted themselves out as tracklayers for the phony company and earned huge profits, bribing several Congressmen and even Grant's vice president, **Schuyler Colfax**, to keep quiet about Crédit Mobilier's unlawful profiteering. In 1872, the scandal was exposed, and Colfax resigned. Again, though Grant had not been knowingly involved in the scandal, he suffered a major blow to his political reputation.

THE WHISKEY RING SCANDAL
Two years later, in 1874, Grant was hit by yet another scandal when several federal employees whom he had appointed embezzled millions of dollars of excise tax revenue. The president vowed to hunt down and punish all those involved in the **Whiskey Ring** but was forced to eat his words when he discovered that his own personal secretary was involved in the ring. Although Grant ended up pardoning his secretary, the Whiskey Ring left yet another stain on his presidency.

THE LIBERAL REPUBLICAN PARTY
Fed up with scandals in the Grant administration, a significant number of Republicans broke ranks with the radicals and moderates in Congress before the 1872 presidential elections, forming a breakaway party called the **Liberal Republican Party**. These congressmen wanted to put an end to governmental corruption, restore the Union, and downsize the federal government.

The Liberal Republicans were largely businessmen, professionals, reformers, and intellectuals who disliked big government and preferred a *laissez-faire* economic policy. Some historians argue that the Liberal Republicans opposed democracy; indeed, they did not support universal manhood suffrage or the enfranchisement of blacks. They also believed that the widespread corruption and graft in American big business and politics were the result of too much democracy and governmental interference.

THE ELECTION OF 1872

The Liberal Republicans nominated *New York Tribune* editor **Horace Greeley** as their candidate for president. The Democratic Party also nominated Greeley as their candidate, because he opposed the army's presence in the South and wanted to end Reconstruction. Radical and moderate Republicans once again nominated Ulysses S. Grant, despite all the scandals during his term. Grant won the election, 286 electoral votes to Greeley's 66, and took the popular vote by a margin of more than 700,000.

THE DEPRESSION OF 1873

Grant's second term was as difficult as his first, this time due to economic problems rather than scandals. During the economic boom of his first term, Americans had taken out too many bad loans and overspeculated in the railroad and business industries. This activity led to the **Depression of 1873,** the first major economic collapse in U.S. history. The depression lasted for roughly five years, and millions of Americans lost their jobs.

THE RESUMPTION ACT OF 1875

In response to dire economic conditions, the poor clamored for cheaper paper and silver money to combat day-to-day hardships. Afraid of driving up inflation, however, Republicans in Congress stopped coining silver dollars in 1873 and passed the **Resumption Act of 1875** to remove all paper money from the economy. These economic policies helped end the depression in the long run but made the interim years more difficult for many Americans.

THE END OF RADICAL RECONSTRUCTION

The Depression of 1873 was politically damaging to radical and moderate Republicans in Congress. Many long-time supporters of the Republican Party, especially in the North, voted Democrat in the congressional **election of 1874**, angry that radical and moderate Republicans adhered so rigidly to hard-money policies even when unemployment in the United States reached nearly fifteen percent.

These northern votes, combined with white votes in the South, ousted many Republicans from Congress and gave the Democratic Party control of the House of Representatives for the first time since 1856. The remaining Radical Republicans in Congress who had not lost their seats suddenly found themselves in the minority party, unable to pass any further legislation concerning southern Reconstruction efforts. The 1874 elections thus marked the beginning of the end of Radical Reconstruction.

The End of Reconstruction: 1873–1877

Events	
1873	Depression of 1873 hits Supreme Court hears Slaughterhouse Cases
1874	Democrats become majority party in House of Representatives
1875	Civil Rights Act of 1875 passed
1876	Samuel J. Tilden and Rutherford B. Hayes both claim victory in presidential election
1877	Congress passes Electoral Count Act Hayes becomes president Hayes removes remaining troops from the South to end Reconstruction

Key People

Rutherford B. Hayes Ohio governor chosen to run against Democrat Samuel J. Tilden in the presidential election of 1876; received fewer popular and electoral votes than Tilden but became president after Compromise of 1877

Samuel J. Tilden Famous New York prosecutor; ran for president on Democratic ticket against Rutherford B. Hayes in election of 1876; fell one electoral vote shy of becoming president

Waning Interest in Reconstruction

As the **Depression of 1873** wore on into the mid-1870s, northern voters became decreasingly interested in southern Reconstruction. With unemployment high and hard currency scarce, northerners were more concerned with their own financial well-being than in securing rights for freedmen, punishing the Ku Klux Klan, or readmitting secessionist states. After Democrats capitalized on these depression conditions and took control of the House of Representatives in 1874, Reconstruction efforts stalled.

The Civil Rights Act of 1875

The Radical Republicans' last successful piece of legislation in Congress was the **Civil Rights Act of 1875**. The bill aimed to eliminate social discrimination and forbade discrimination in all public places, such as theaters, hotels, and restaurants. The bill stated that blacks should be treated as equals under the law and that they could sue violators of the law in federal court.

Unfortunately, the act proved ineffective, as Democrats in the House made sure the bill was unenforceable. The act stated that blacks had to file claims to defend their own rights; the federal government could not do it for them. Many blacks were still poor and worked hard to make a living, and House Democrats knew that lawsuits would require money and considerable effort.

DEMOCRATS TAKE THE SOUTH

Meanwhile, Democrats were steadily regaining control of the South, as the already-weak Republican presence in region only became weaker as northerners lost interest in Reconstruction. The Depression of 1873, along with continued pressure from the **Ku Klux Klan**, drove most white Unionists, **carpetbaggers**, and **scalawags** out of the South by the mid-1870s, leaving blacks alone to fight for radical legislation. Democrats regained their seats in state legislatures, beginning with majorities in Virginia and Tennessee in 1869 and moving steadily onward to other states. Many Democrats used violence to secure power, and several Republicans were murdered in Mississippi in the 1875 elections. Blacks continued to be terrorized and intimidated into not voting. By 1877, Democrats had majorities in every southern state.

THE SLAUGHTERHOUSE CASES

The shift of political power in the South was only one cause of the end of Radical Reconstruction. The other key factor was a series of sweeping Supreme Court rulings in the 1870s and 1880s that weakened radical policy in the years before. The first of these were the 1873 **Slaughterhouse Cases**, so named because they involved a suit against a New Orleans slaughterhouse. In these cases, the conservative Supreme Court ruled that the Fourteenth Amendment protected U.S. citizens from rights infringements only on a federal level, not on a state level.

UNITED STATES V. CRUIKSHANK

Moreover, in 1876, the Supreme Court ruled in *United States v. Cruikshank* that only states, not the federal government, could prosecute individuals under the Ku Klux Klan Act of 1871. As a result, countless Klan crimes went unpunished by southern state governments, who tacitly condoned the violence.

The final nail in the coffin was the Civil Rights Cases of 1883. In these rulings, the Court further declared the Civil Rights Act of 1875 unconstitutional, saying that the Fourteenth Amendment applied only to discrimination from the government, not from individuals. Collectively, these rulings from the Supreme Court, along with the Democratic Party's political resurgence in the South, brought an end to Radical Reconstruction.

THE ELECTION OF 1876

In 1876, the Democratic Party, having already secured a majority in the South, made a concerted effort to win the White House as well. The party nominated the famous Grant-era prosecutor **Samuel J. Tilden** as their presidential hopeful. After briefly thinking about re-nominating Ulysses S. Grant for an unprecedented third term, Republicans instead nominated Ohio Governor **Rutherford B. Hayes**. Even though Hayes was a relative unknown, Republicans thought of him as the perfect candidate: he had been a Union general in the Civil War, had no controversial opinions, and came from a politically important state. In the election, Tilden received 184 electoral votes of the 185 needed to become president. Hayes only received 165 votes and lost the popular vote by approximately 250,000 votes.

However, the election results were disputed because of confusing ballots in South Carolina, Louisiana, and Florida. Under normal procedure, disputed votes would be recounted in front of Congress by the president of the Senate. However, the president of the Senate was a Republican and the Speaker of the House was a Democrat, so neither man could be trusted to count the votes fairly.

THE COMPROMISE OF 1877

Congress therefore passed the **Electoral Count Act** in 1877 to establish a special committee to recount the votes in a fair and balanced way. The committee consisted of fifteen men from the House, Senate, and Supreme Court. The committee concluded by a margin of one vote that the Republican Hayes had won the disputed states and therefore was the new president. Democrats were outraged at first but quickly realized that the situation gave them the perfect opportunity to strike a bargain with the opposition to achieve their political goals.

The result was the **Compromise of 1877**, in which Democrats agreed to let Hayes become president in exchange for a complete withdrawal of federal troops from the South. Republicans agreed, and shortly after Hayes was sworn in as president, he ordered the remaining federal troops to vacate South Carolina and Louisiana.

REASONS FOR THE END OF RECONSTRUCTION

Ultimately, Reconstruction ended because of several factors. Northerners were tired of a decade of Reconstruction efforts and had become less interested in the South with the rise of speculation and profit-making in the Gilded Age and then the hardships of the Depression of 1873. In addition, the conservative Supreme Court repeatedly struck down Radical Republican legislation, issuing rulings that had a devastating effect on blacks' civil liberties. Meanwhile, the persistent scare tactics of the Ku Klux Klan and other southern white groups drove many Republicans out of office, giving Democrats a majority in every southern state by 1877. Finally, the **Compromise of 1877** and removal of the remaining federal troops from the South signaled the end of the Reconstruction era.

THE SUCCESSES OF RECONSTRUCTION

Reconstruction was a success in the sense that America, after 1877, could once again be called the United States. All of the southern states had drafted new constitutions; ratified the Thirteenth, Fourteenth, and Fifteenth Amendments; and pledged loyalty to the Union. Together, the Civil War and Reconstruction also settled the states' fights vs. federalism debate that had been going on since the Virginia and Kentucky Resolutions of the 1790s and the Nullification Crisis of the 1830s. As one historian noted, the United States before the Civil War *were* a country, but the United States after the war *was* a nation.

THE FAILURES OF RECONSTRUCTION

However, although Reconstruction was a success in a broad sense, it was a failure in several specific ways. The swift changes in political power in the South rendered useless most of the legislation that Radical Republicans had passed through Congress. Rutherford B. Hayes's removal of federal troops from the South in 1877 allowed many former Confederates and slave owners to regain power, and this return of power to whites also meant a return to the policy of the old South. Southern politicians passed the black codes and voter qualifications and allowed the sharecropping system to thrive—all with the support of a conservative U.S. Supreme Court, whose key court rulings in the 1870s and 1880s effectively repealed the Fourteenth and Fifteenth Amendments and the Civil Rights Act of 1875.

As a result, by 1877, northerners were tired of Reconstruction; weary of battling southern elites, scandal, and radicalism; and had largely lost interest in supporting black civil rights. Theoretically, North and South reached a compromise: black civil liberties and racial equality would be set aside in order to put the Union back together. As it turned out, blacks would not regain the support of the federal government until the civil rights movement of the 1960s.

STUDY QUESTIONS & ESSAY TOPICS

Always use specific historical examples to support your arguments.

STUDY QUESTIONS

1. *In what ways was Reconstruction a success? A failure? Explain.*

Reconstruction was a success in that it restored the United States as a unified nation: by 1877, all of the former Confederate states had drafted new constitutions, acknowledged the Thirteenth, Fourteenth, and Fifteenth Amendments, and pledged their loyalty to the U.S. government. Reconstruction also finally settled the states' rights vs. federalism debate that had been an issue since the 1790s.

However, Reconstruction failed by most other measures: Radical Republican legislation ultimately failed to protect former slaves from white persecution and failed to engender fundamental changes to the social fabric of the South. When President Rutherford B. Hayes removed federal troops from the South in 1877, former Confederate officials and slave owners almost immediately returned to power. With the support of a conservative Supreme Court, these newly empowered white southern politicians passed black codes, voter qualifications, and other anti-progressive legislation to reverse the rights that blacks had gained during Radical Reconstruction. The U.S. Supreme Court bolstered this anti-progressive movement with decisions in the Slaughterhouse Cases, the Civil Rights Cases, and *United States v. Cruikshank* that effectively repealed the Fourteenth and Fifteenth Amendments and the Civil Rights Act of 1875.

Meanwhile, the sharecropping system—essentially a legal form of slavery that kept blacks tied to land owned by rich white farmers—became widespread in the South. With little economic power, blacks ended up having to fight for civil rights on their own, as northern whites lost interest in Reconstruction by the mid-1870s. By 1877, northerners were tired of Reconstruction, scandals, radicals, and the fight for blacks' rights. Reconstruction thus came to a close with many of its goals left unaccomplished.

2. *Some historians have suggested that had Lincoln not
    been assassinated, Radical Republicans in the House
    might have impeached him instead of Andrew Johnson.
    Defend this argument.*

Radical Republicans in Congress might have impeached President
Lincoln after the Civil War, had he not been assassinated, because he
and Congress had contrasting visions for handling postwar Reconstruction. Ultimately, however, Congress ended up impeaching
President Andrew Johnson, who followed many parts of Lincoln's
blueprint for Reconstruction.

In 1863, Lincoln wanted to end the Civil War as quickly as possible. He feared that strong northern public support for the war
would wane if the fighting continued and knew that the war was
also taking an enormous toll on northern families and resources.
Lincoln worried that if the war dragged on, a settlement would be
reached that would leave the North and South as two separate
nations. As it turned out, his fears were justified: by late 1863, an
increasing number of Democrats were calling for a truce and peaceful resolution to the conflict.

As a result, in the Proclamation of Amnesty and Reconstruction
of 1863, Lincoln drafted lenient specifications for secessionist states
for readmission into the Union—an attempt to entice Unionists and
those tired of fighting in the South to surrender. His Ten-Percent
Plan, part of the proclamation, called for southern states to be readmitted into the Union after 10 percent of the voting public swore a
loyalty oath to the United States. In addition, he offered to pardon
all Confederate officials and pledged to protect southerners' private
property. Lincoln did not want Reconstruction to be a long, drawn-
out process; rather, he wanted the states to draft new constitutions
so that the Union could be quickly restored.

Radical Republicans, on the other hand, wanted the South to pay
a price for secession and believed that Congress, not the president,
should direct the process of Reconstruction. The Radical Republicans saw serious flaws in Civil War–era southern society and were
adamant that the South needed full social rehabilitation to resemble
the North. Many Republican Congressmen also aimed to improve
education and labor conditions to benefit all of the oppressed classes
in southern society, black and white. To quicken this transformation
of the South, Congress passed a series of progressive legislation,
including the Civil Rights Act of 1866, the First and Second Recon-

struction Acts, the Ku Klux Klan Act of 1871, the Civil Rights Act of 1875, and the Thirteenth, Fourteenth, and Fifteenth Amendments to the U.S. Constitution.

In the end, Radical Republicans in the House impeached President Andrew Johnson in 1868 because he repeatedly blocked their attempt to pass radical legislation. For example, Johnson vetoed the Civil Rights Act of 1866, the Freedmen's Bureau charter, and the ratification of the Fourteenth Amendment, all of which were progressive, "radical" bills. Had Lincoln remained alive, he might have been in the same position himself: he wanted Reconstruction to end quickly and did not necessarily favor progressive legislation. Indeed, Lincoln had made it clear during the Civil War that he was fighting to restore the Union, not to emancipate slaves. It is likely that Lincoln thus would have battled with Congress over the control of Reconstruction, blocked key Reconstruction policies, and met as vindictive a House as Johnson did 1868.

3. Explain how three of the following shaped northern politics during Reconstruction:
    a) black codes
    b) the Depression of 1873
    c) Crédit Mobilier
    d) the "Swing Around the Circle" speeches
    e) the Resumption Act of 1875

The Crédit Mobilier scandal, the Depression of 1873, and the Resumption Act of 1875 focused attention away from the South and onto political and economic woes in the North. All three thus played a role in ending Reconstruction.

In the 1860s, executives of the Union Pacific Railroad created a dummy construction company called Crédit Mobilier and then hired themselves out as contractors at high rates to earn large profits. The executives bribed dozens of Congressmen and cabinet members in Ulysses S. Grant's administration, including Grant's vice president, to allow the scam to work. The scheme was eventually exposed, and many politicians were forced to resign. Along with other scandals, such as the Fisk-Gould gold scandal and the Whiskey Ring, Crédit Mobilier distracted northern voters' attention away from southern Reconstruction and toward corruption and graft problems in the North.

When the Depression of 1873 struck, northern voters became even less interested in pursuing Reconstruction efforts. Unemployment climbed to 15 percent, and hard currency became scarce. With pressing economic problems, northerners did not have time to worry about helping former slaves, punishing the Ku Klux Klan, or readmitting southern states into the Union.

Moreover, the Republican Party's adherence to unpopular, strict monetary policies in response to the depression—such as the Resumption Act of 1875—opened the door for the Democratic Party to make large political gains, accelerating the end of Reconstruction. The Resumption Act reduced the amount of currency circulating in the economy in an effort to curb inflation caused by the depression. Although the act improved economic conditions in the long run, it made for harder times in both the North and South in the short run. The Act was Republican-sponsored, so Democrats were able to capitalize on its unpopularity to rally support for their party. This increased popularity translated into election victories that enabled Democrats to retake the South, bringing Reconstruction to a close.

Suggested Essay Topics

1. *Compare and contrast Lincoln's plans for Reconstruction, Presidential Reconstruction, and Radical Reconstruction.*

2. *What effect did Reconstruction have on blacks? Were they better off after Reconstruction than they were before the Civil War?*

3. *Was the impeachment of President Johnson justified? Why or why not? What were the consequences of his acquittal in the Senate?*

4. *What effect did the Compromise of 1877 have on politics in the North and South?*

REVIEW & RESOURCES

QUIZ

1. The 1863 Proclamation of Amnesty and Reconstruction proposed

    A. A plan for Radical Reconstruction
    B. The Ten-Percent Plan
    C. The Fifty-Percent Plan
    D. Andrew Johnson's Plan for Reconstruction

2. Why did Congress reject Louisiana's new constitution in 1864?

    A. It was drafted according to the Ten-Percent Plan
    B. It gave blacks the right to vote
    C. Congressmen believed it was too early to begin readmitting states
    D. All of the above

3. The Wade-Davis Bill stipulated that states could reenter the Union

    A. When 10 percent of voters pledged allegiance
    B. When 50 percent of voters pledged allegiance
    C. Only after ratifying the Fourteenth Amendment
    D. Only after ratifying the Fifteenth Amendment

4. Why did Lincoln pocket-veto the Wade-Davis Bill?

    A. He did not want slaves to have the right to vote
    B. He thought it was too early to begin Reconstruction
    C. He thought the bill was too lenient on white southerners
    D. He thought it would ruin his chance for reelection

5. The Radical Republicans

    A. Were only a minority group in Congress
    B. Wanted to punish the South for secession and the war
    C. Wanted to protect the civil and political rights of blacks
    D. All of the above

6. The Freedmen's Bureau had the most success in

    A. Establishing schools for blacks
    B. Redistributing land to former slaves
    C. Distributing food and supplies to blacks and poor whites
    D. Safeguarding blacks' civil liberties

7. The Compromise of 1877 was reached after

    A. Samuel J. Tilden conceded to Rutherford B. Hayes
    B. Congress passed the Electoral Count Act
    C. Congress agreed to repeal the Civil Rights Act of 1875
    D. Congress agreed to repeal the Ku Klux Klan Act

8. All of the following were components of Lincoln's blueprint for Reconstruction *except*

    A. Readmission to the Union when 10 percent of voters pledged their allegiance to the United States
    B. A promise to protect all private property, excluding slaves
    C. Black suffrage
    D. Full pardons for all white southerners, except high-ranking military and government officials

9. What did William Tecumseh Sherman's Special Field Order No. 15 do?

    A. Emancipated all blacks whom his soldiers encountered in the South
    B. Set aside land in Georgia and South Carolina specifically for freed slaves
    C. Established the Freedmen's Bureau
    D. Established martial law in Georgia according to the First Reconstruction Act

10. The Thirteenth Amendment

    A. Prohibited slavery
    B. Granted citizenship to all Americans regardless of race
    C. Enfranchised all American men
    D. Prohibited presidents from serving more than two full terms

11. The Civil Rights Act of 1866 extended all of the following liberties to black Americans *except*

    A. The right to testify against whites
    B. The right to serve on juries
    C. The right to enter into legal contracts
    D. The right to vote

12. Which constitutional amendment did the Civil Rights Act of 1866 most closely resemble?

    A. The Twelfth Amendment
    B. The Thirteenth Amendment
    C. The Fourteenth Amendment
    D. The Fifteenth Amendment

13. What effect did the 1866 Memphis and New Orleans race riots and Andrew Johnson's "Swing Around the Circle" speeches have?

    A. Convinced northerners that racism could never be completely eliminated
    B. Encouraged northerners to vote Democrat
    C. Encouraged northerners to vote Republican
    D. Divided the North between those who wanted harsher Reconstruction and those who wanted to end Reconstruction

14. Which U.S. Supreme Court decision(s) did the Fourteenth Amendment reverse?

    A. The Slaughterhouse Cases
    B. The Civil Rights Cases
    C. Dred Scott v. Sanford
    D. United States v. Cruikshank

REVIEW & RESOURCES

15. Andrew Johnson believed that

    A. Blacks should be given the right to vote
    B. Blacks should be citizens
    C. Southern society should be completely transformed
    D. None of the above

16. By 1880, most southern blacks had found employment as

    A. Sharecroppers
    B. Artisans
    C. Landowners of small farms
    D. Wage laborers

17. Southern legislatures passed the black codes in response to

    A. Depression of 1873
    B. The Civil Rights Act of 1866
    C. The Fourteenth Amendment
    D. The Civil Rights Act of 1875

18. Who were carpetbaggers?

    A. Northern whites who moved to the South after the war
    B. White planter elites in the South
    C. Southern black politicians
    D. Northern Democrats who opposed Radical Reconstruction

19. Who were scalawags?

    A. Northern whites who moved to the South after the war
    B. White Unionists in the South
    C. Southern black politicians
    D. Northern Democrats who opposed Radical Reconstruction

20. The Ku Klux Klan was founded in Tennessee after the passage of the

    A. Fourteenth Amendment
    B. Fifteenth Amendment
    C. Civil Rights Act of 1875
    D. Civil Rights Act of 1866

21. After the Civil War, many former slaves celebrated their freedom by

    A. Searching for and reuniting with family members
    B. Pressing for education for their children
    C. Marrying
    D. All of the above

22. Why did most southern blacks prefer sharecropping to wage labor after the Civil War?

    A. Wages were too low to support their families
    B. They preferred the autonomy of farming their own plots
    C. Jobs with wages were competitive, but sharecropping was easy
    D. Not even whites wanted to be wage laborers

23. Why did southern white landowners prefer the sharecropping system to wage labor after the Civil War?

    A. Paying wage laborers was too expensive
    B. They made more money off the sharecropping system
    C. Sharecropping kept blacks bound to servitude as agricultural laborers
    D. Sharecropping required less work

24. One consequence of the Depression of 1873 was that

    A. Democrats regained control of the House of Representatives
    B. Republicans lost the White House in 1876
    C. Liberal Republicans split from the moderates and radicals
    D. All of the above

25. Liberal Republicans fought for all of the following *except*

    A. An end to Reconstruction
    B. Black suffrage
    C. Reform
    D. Downsizing the federal government

REVIEW & RESOURCES

26. Who nominated Horace Greeley for president in 1872?

    A. Moderate and Radical Republicans
    B. Democrats
    C. The Union Party
    D. Democrats and Liberal Republicans

27. What was Crédit Mobilier?

    A. A dummy construction company created by corrupt railroad executives
    B. A scheme to embezzle funds from the U.S. Treasury
    C. A plot to corner the gold market
    D. A New York City corruption ring

28. Samuel J. Tilden rose to national fame when he

    A. Exposed the Whiskey Ring
    B. Prosecuted William "Boss" Tweed
    C. Ran for Congress as a Liberal Republican
    D. Ran for vice president as Horace Greeley's running mate

29. Liberal Republicans rose to power primarily because many northerners wanted

    A. To end Military Reconstruction
    B. More protection for blacks' civil liberties
    C. To get Grant out of office
    D. To end widespread corruption within the government

30. The Depression of 1873 was caused by all of the following *except*

    A. Bad bank loans
    B. Overspeculation in manufacturing
    C. Overspeculation in railroads
    D. Fears that the federal government was on the verge of bankruptcy

31. President Grant is best described as

    A. A corrupt politician who misused government funds and privileges
    B. An apathetic president who only wanted the spoils of office
    C. An honest but politically inexperienced man
    D. A diehard Radical Republican

32. Which of the following was one of the fastest-growing sectors of the economy during the Reconstruction era?

    A. Railroads
    B. Cotton
    C. Shipping
    D. Telecommunications

33. The government officials who embezzled money from the U.S. Treasury in 1874 were known as the

    A. Tweed Ring
    B. Crédit Mobilier
    C. Whiskey Ring
    D. Gold Ring

34. The Civil Rights Act of 1875 was a failure for all of the following reasons *except*

    A. Only individuals could file claims against violators
    B. Military Reconstruction ended before the bill was passed
    C. House Democrats had weakened the bill
    D. It was too difficult to enforce

35. What brought on the end of Radical Reconstruction?

    A. Democrats' rise to power in Congress in 1874
    B. President Hayes's removal of federal troops from the South in 1877
    C. The Civil Rights Act of 1875
    D. The Liberal Republicans' split from the moderates and radicals in 1872

REVIEW & RESOURCES

36. Which law did Congress pass to try to outlaw racial discrimination in all public places?

    A. Fourteenth Amendment
    B. Fifteenth Amendment
    C. Civil Rights Act of 1866
    D. Civil Rights Act of 1875

37. The Supreme Court's ruling in the 1873 Slaughterhouse Cases weakened blacks' rights under the

    A. Fourteenth Amendment
    B. Fifteenth Amendment
    C. Civil Rights Act of 1866
    D. Civil Rights Act of 1875

38. Democrats allowed Rutherford B. Hayes to become president in 1877 when Republicans promised to

    A. Repeal the Civil Rights Act of 1875
    B. Withdraw all federal troops from the South
    C. Overlook acts of terror by the Ku Klux Klan
    D. Print cheap paper money to assist impoverished farmers

39. What did the Compromise of 1877 do?

    A. Put a Republican in the White House
    B. Ended black dreams of racial equality
    C. Ended Reconstruction
    D. All of the above

40. The Supreme Court ruled in *United States v. Cruikshank* that

    A. The Civil Rights Act of 1875 was unconstitutional
    B. Racial discrimination by the federal government was illegal
    C. Only states could prosecute violators of the Ku Klux Klan Act of 1871
    D. Southern states could establish voter qualification requirements

41. Radicals in the House impeached Andrew Johnson in 1868 because he had violated the

    A. Civil Rights Act of 1866
    B. Electoral Count Act
    C. Resumption Act
    D. Tenure of Office Act

42. What did the Fourteenth Amendment do?

    A. Forbade slavery
    B. Granted citizenship to black Americans
    C. Gave black men the right to vote
    D. Forbade racial discrimination in public places

43. What did the Fifteenth Amendment do?

    A. Forbade slavery
    B. Granted citizenship to black Americans
    C. Gave all men the right to vote
    D. Forbade racial discrimination in public places

44. Why did seven Republican senators vote with Democrats to acquit Andrew Johnson during his impeachment trial?

    A. They did not want the president *pro tempore* of the Senate to replace Johnson
    B. They did not want to establish a dangerous precedent
    C. They did not believe the charges were substantial enough to warrant his removal from office
    D. All of the above

45. The First Reconstruction Act did all of the following *except*

    A. Divide the South into five military districts
    B. Declare that the southern states were to be treated as conquered territories
    C. Establish martial law in the South
    D. Place federal troops in charge of voter registration

46. All of the following are reasons that Republicans nominated Rutherford B. Hayes for president in 1876 *except*

    A. He had served two terms as a senator
    B. He was from the politically important state of Ohio
    C. He had no controversial political opinions
    D. He had been a Union general in the Civil War

47. From which group did southern Republicans received most of their support?

    A. Unionist whites
    B. Blacks
    C. Wealthy white landowners
    D. The Ku Klux Klan

48. Congress passed the Resumption Act in 1875 to

    A. Control the Ku Klux Klan
    B. Withdraw federal troops from the South
    C. Reduce the amount of money in circulation
    D. Control white "redeemer" governments in the South

49. Grant's reputation was damaged by all of the following scandals *except*

    A. The Crédit Mobilier scandal
    B. The Fisk-Gould scheme
    C. The Whiskey Ring
    D. The Tweed Ring

50. Grant is buried in

    A.   Washington's Tomb
    B.   Jefferson's Tomb
    C.   Lincoln's Tomb
    D.   Grant's Tomb

ANSWER KEY

1. b; 2. a; 3. b; 4. d; 5. d; 6. a; 7. b; 8. c; 9. b; 10. a; 11. d; 12. c; 13. c;
14. c; 15. d; 16. a; 17. b; 18. a; 19. b; 20. b; 21. d; 22. b; 23. c; 24. a;
25. b; 26. d; 27. a; 28. b; 29. d; 30. d; 31. d; 32. a; 33. c; 34. b; 35. a;
36. d; 37. a; 38. b; 39. b; 40. c; 41. c; 42. b; 43. c; 44. d; 45. d; 46. a;
47. b; 48. c; 49. d; 50. d

SUGGESTIONS FOR FURTHER READING

CIMBALA, PAUL A., AND RANDALL M. MILLER, EDS. *The Freedmen's Bureau and Reconstruction: Reconsiderations.* New York: Fordham University Press, 1999.

FONER, ERIC. *Reconstruction: America's Unfinished Revolution, 1863–1877.* New York: Perennial, 2002.

LABBE, RONALD M., AND JONATHAN LURIE. *The Slaughterhouse Cases: Regulation, Reconstruction, and the Fourteenth Amendment.* Lawrence: University Press of Kansas, 2003.

SMITH, JEAN EDWARD. *Grant.* New York: Simon and Schuster, 2001.

STAMPP, KENNETH M. *The Era of Reconstruction, 1865–1877.* New York: Vintage Press, 1967.

TREFOUSSE, HANS LOUIS. *Impeachment of a President: Andrew Johnson, the Blacks, and Reconstruction.* New York: Fordham University Press, 1999.

REVIEW & RESOURCES